They Told Me Not To Tell

DOZIER REFORM SCHOOL A LIVING HELL

JOHNNY LEE GADDY

ACKNOWLEDGMENTS

First and most importantly I want to thank God Almighty that I made it out alive to talk about the abuse I suffered at Arthur G. Dozier Reform School. I want to thank my loving and supportive wife Josephine for all her support and encouragement. I want to thank my daughter Catina for all the hard work and long hours she spent working with Antoinette Harrell to get my book published. I want to give a special thanks to Antoinette Harrell for her dedicated and committed support helping me to bring my story to the media. Special thanks also to Adjunct Professor Clare Washington at Portland State University for teaching a class on the abuse that took place at Arthur G. Dozier Reform School. I want to thank Walter C. Black, Sr., for taking the photographs for this book. Joelle Kennedy LaCoste and Imani Blossom for their artwork. Art Rocker for his support. Roger Kiser Dean for blowing the whistle about the abuse at Dozier. Andrew Puel and Robert Straley for their long hours of research.

FORWORD

Antoinette Harrell interviews the author, Johnny Lee Gaddy, as he talks about his experience as a youth in the 1950s; and being incarcerated at what was supposed to be a school to educate and reform young wayward boys --sent there through the juvenile justice court system. Dozier School for Boys in Marianna, Florida, did anything but *reform* Johnny Lee Gaddy or any other boy who spent time within its walls and compound. Gaddy tells his story about his experiences and the time he spent at Dozier School for Boys, in a very honest and poignant manner, through various interview sessions. Effectively blending the context and the complicated circumstances of the story makes this book simply extraordinarily fascinating and educative.

Particularly fascinating is the fact that the themes of the book address real life past and present issues. The chapter titled *Child Labor*, Harrell asks Gaddy to tell her about the labor he did while at Dozier Reform School. Gaddy reminisces about being awakened about 5:30 a.m. in the morning by a bugle; and then being taken out to the swamp to clear the ground to plant corn, as he was one of the farm crew. *"The even days we went to work, the odd days we went to school,"* Gaddy muses. Not getting up at the sound of the bugle to begin the morning chores or any other Infringement on the rules of Dozier Reform School, meant a trip to the "White House" – not the infamous White House where the nation's president resides in Washington, D.C., but the building that helped breed fear and even the desire to endure death, rather than undergo the punishment meted out by the staff once you were sent there. In the chapter titled *Dozier Reform School was a Living Hell*, Gaddy reveals even more real-life atrocities that he and other young boys endured while being committed to Dozier. In one of the interviews, Harrell asks, *"Johnny could you please tell me why would you describe Dozier Reform School as a 'living hell'?* And Gaddy responds, *"Well, because of the work that we had to do and the conditions that we had to do it in."* Even more interesting is Gaddy's craftiness in setting all the horrible experiences against the beautiful scenery that one sees upon entering the grounds of Dozier, confirming the utter disbelief that such dark and evil deeds were being done to young, innocent boys sent there to be reformed in order to re-enter society as future model citizens.

Antoinette tells the rest of the story about how some of these boys were found many years later in unmarked graves in 2014, on the grounds of what was Dozier School for Boys.

This book reminds me of many courses in Black Studies , especially courses such as my own on "African Americans and 20th Century Slavery", about those who had been left behind – even after the signing of the Emancipation Proclamation — left on plantations and enslaved way into the twentieth and twenty-first century. Antoinette Harrell's writing was very instrumental in my decision to teach this course, as she was and still is a constant source for my course material. Harrell reminds us all about the plight of so many young men who had been kept at Dozier School for Boys (or Dozier Reform School), and how they compare well to those who were enslaved and treated as inhumanely before and after the signing of the Emancipation Proclamation. I highly recommend Johnny Lee Gaddy's book to further educate for the benefit of our students, on the evils of slavery, and especially how in the twentieth century, these young boys who were incarcerated at Dozier were still enslaved.

They should have been free, in their circumstances to grow up and be all that they could be, with fond childhood memories

6– instead of memories of the school of horrors exceeded only by some of the staff that were in charge.

The fascination of the perfect blend of these testimonies await all students, scholars and communities in this most educational and educative book. It is truly extraordinary and highly recommended.

Clare J. Washington

Black Studies

Portland State University

CONTENTS

CHAPTER ONE

THEY MADE ME DO IT

If you don't... if you turn that bed over, there's a probablity I can kill you because I can hit you in your testicles and it might kill you, so you better hold that bed."

Antoinette: Johnny would you please tell me what was some of the things they made you do?

Johnny: I mostly done field work on the farm.

Antoniette: Can we talk about how you were molested?

Johnny: It was doing the night when the boys got ready to go to bed. He would come to the cottage and tell the cottage father that he was taken us to the library or something like that. That when he would take us to an area and molest us. Sometimes, it was about six different boys in the course of a month or whenever he got ready to. I don't know his name.

Antoinette: Tell me about the time you was molested and who molested you. I can't remember the man's name who raped me.

Johnny: Well, it was horribly because it was something that I didn't want to do, and something that I really didn't like, but they made me do it,

Antoinette: Did they tell you not to tell?

Johnny: Yes, they definitely told me not to tell, they'll threaten my life if I told anybody so I was scared all of the time so I definitely wouldn't tell no one.

Antoinette: Can you tell me what you remember about the rape?

Johnny: The first time when it happened?

Antoinette: Yes, hmhmm,

Johnny: Well when he called me I was in Robinson cottage and I didn't tell anyone that he told me to clean the office, he told me to take off all of my clothes and I asked why should I take off my clothes? Thats when he got physical and started hitting on me.

Antoinette: Who beat you or spanked you?

The black guy named Marvin and I think his name was Marvin and I can't remember his first name. You know, he told me that I'm going to have you destroyed and you know somebody could beat you up pretty bad.

Antoinette: Did he beat you up?

Johnny: I got abuse and hit.

Johnny: The rapist would come around to the cottages. He would come around the cottage and tell the boys that he was training boys how to keep silent about the abuse and stuff like like. He had a key to get in the cottage. I believe the cottage father knew that he was abusing the boys.

Antoinette: Did he beat you up on your first encounter?

Johnny: Well, no he didn't beat me up, but I was scared to death so I submitted to what he wanted me to do.

Antoinette: Was that the first time? And did he come back after that?

11

Johnny: No, that wasn't the first time. He did come back several times later. When he came back a couple of times later he would repeated the same act again? He came back for others also. I told my cottage father about it and he knew what was going on and he said, "You know what they would do too you if you told somebody." He said, "you need to quit lying because you can get yourself in some trouble by lying on a person like that." I just said, "I wouldn't lie," he said I tell you what, I'm going to ask the director, and I'm going to see what you have to say then. He denied it so he told me I should stop lying and going around telling somebody lies like that . So I knew right then I didn't have no one to talk to. He theatren my life for telling the truth, they told me that they would kill everyone in my family. I was scared to death all of the time. I didn't have anyone to trust, but you didn't know who to tell, telling would just make the situation worse and he could really hurt you.

Antoinette: What age was you at that time when he first came to you and molested you?

Johnny: 11 years old.

Antoinette: Did the other boys report what happened to them?

Johnny No, but I did. The boys didn't say anything about it, but I got to say some of the boys that I knew left the cottage and they didn't come back.

I don't know what happened to them. I can say they were hurting, he did nasty things. He was really nasty. He could hurt you. He could hurt you really bad. He did some pretty bad things to the boys, he was crazy and we knew he was that way and that's what I am saying. All of the directors around knew and they just covered up for him. They covered up for him all the time.

Antoinette: A couple of years ago, I interviewed you, you told me that this was the very first time that you discussed this with someone. Why did you carried this around with you for so long without saying a word to anyone?

Johnny: I guess I was just really embarrassed to say what happened thats not something that I wanted to go around and talk about, really because I never mentioned that to my wife, but she said she figured it out. She has some idea that it happened to me and I didn't know how she felt. She figured it out , but its lot of things, the way she touched me that made me uncomfortable.

Antoinette: Did you tell your mother you was molested?

Johnny: No. I never mentioned it. No, you're the first one that I ever mentioned that to.

Antoinette: Why didn't you tell your mother?

Johnny: No one believed me, not even my mother.

Antoinette: I know that had to be a disappoint to you.

Johnny: I think the lot of us have big egos or we're very embarrassed by it. For a man to be raped and talk about it, its very embarrassing. We were kids and we were scared to death.

Antoinette: Is there anyone else that you can remember who molested the boys ?

Johnny: No, I know a little boy who was molested, his name was ? King; I have been trying to find about him and what happened to him. I don't want to call his name for privacy issues.

Antoinette: You said ? King or ? King. Okay.

Johnny: We both stayed in Robinson cottage.

Antoinette: How do you know that he was molested?

Johnny: Because he came back bleeding that night everybody knew something happened. It was an open space and the boy walked in the room crying. He had only been at Dozier for a couple months.

Antoinette: Was he bleeding from the rectum?

Johnny: Yes,

Antoinette: How could you all tell that?

Johnny: Well, he came in and went to the bathroom and that's how we knew that something happened. You can see the blood on his clothes. The cottage father made him take a shower.

Antoinette: Are you saying the person who raped the boys would who make the boys take shower afterward?

Johnny: The cottage father would tell you to take a shower, he knew what that man was doing to the boys always, he took advantage of the boys.

Antoinette: Was any of the boys younger then you?

Johnny: There was boys about eight years old.

Johnny: You can hear the boys in the bed screaming and crying. Some crying at night almost every night they were lying there crying.

Antoinette: Why were they crying ?

Johnny: Some was crying because they had been molested. That was not the best feeling in your life and they told you that you know you got to man up and that they were boys and need to act like a man. "How could you carry yourself like a man when you was not a man!" Some of them was crying to go home and for family.

Antoinette: You said after you was assaulted they told you to man up?

Johnny: Yeah, you have to man up and think like a man and and not cry like baby. They knew what was going on in that place. Everybody knew what was going on. They just wasn't saying anything and we couldn't talk to them about it.

Antoinette: Did you do whatever they asked to stay alive?

Johnny: Yes, there were bullied in the cottage too.

Antoinette: Was the bullies trying to molest the little boys also?

Johnny: Some of them. Mostly anybody that was weak.

Antoinette: Did any of the boys ever end up going to the hospital after being raped?

Johnny: I really don't know. They're finding out what actually happened now. The whole state of Florida was tied in all of that stuff. But they didn't believe us because we were boys and they would tell people that we were bad boys so no one would believe us or listen to us.

Antoinette: Did they give you the reputation for being dishonest boy and criminal?

Johnny: I didn't go to school because I didn't like the children teasing and picking at me. I had a speech impairment thats all.

Antoinette: Do you think of the horrible acts that took place at the reform school concerning the missing boys and the bodies being exhumed on the school campus?

Johnny: Ms. Harrell, I think about the boys all the time. Sometimes I can be watching something on telelvision about a child or person being raped or beat and I start crying.

Antoinette: Do you think more men will come forward to talk about what happened to them when they were raped?

Johnny: It is so embarrassing for a man to say you were molested by a man, but a lot of them wouldn't say it. I believe that and I hope that they will come forth with the truth.

Antoinette: During a previous interview you said that the rapist would come around and just look in the windows at night and that made you feel very uncomfortable and scared.

Antoinette: Would you tell me about that?

Johnny: Well the boys stayed on the first floor and the cottage father stayed on the second floor. The night watchmen came by he had a key that he inserted in the clock. He came twice a night. I don't know the man name, I know he was and old white man. He would get a head count of all the boys. The man who molested the boys would avoid the night watchman. He came after the night watchman left.

Antoinette: Did this happened all through the week?

Johnny: Not all through the week, but a couple times a month he come by to get different boys.

Antoinette: Is there anything else you want to tell us about these horrible acts?

Antoinette : Did it happen in your sleeping quarters or was it a certain place and location where is the assaults took place?

Johnny: Well, he took me to the gym. They had a gym and sometimes he would take me to his office or around the swimming pool.

Antoinette: Is that the night that you thought you was going to clean up?

Johnny: That's right.

Antoinette: Did the rapist have a family living on the premises or the campus?

Johnny: No. He didn't have family there on the campus.

Antoinette: Did some of the other boys have family living around

Johnny: Yes.

Antoinette: Was you friends with the others little boys who was raped.

Johnny: Yes, I know of other little boys, but I forgot some of their names.

Antoinette: Where there other cottage fathers that was raping boys?

Johnny: No, not in Robinson cottage.

Antoinette: ? You said they mostly raped the little boys when they first got to Dozier.

Johnny: Yes, that's what they did.

Antoinette: You said you was assaulted three to four times.

Johnny: Right.

Antoinette: Are you sure?

Johnny: Yes.

Antoinette: Johnny, I'm so sorry you went through this. I'm so sorry that this interview is making you re-live that horrible experience all over again.

CHAPTER TWO

DOZIER REFORM SCHOOL A LIVING HELL

Well that's how it was worse...it was worse than that because we was always scared because they had a vehicle we call a "Blue Goose", and when they see that Blue Goose coming round on your job or at your cottage you got scared to death.

Antoinette: Johnny would you please tell me why you describe Dozier Reform School as a 'living hell'?

Johnny: Well, because of the work that we had to do and the conditions that we had to live in. Also the conditions we worked in as children, the abuse, rapes and beating we suffered through. Some of those boys were killed.

Antoinette: I interviewed you last year and you described the school as...the campus that was very beautiful and a campus that was so beautiful with lots of trees and the way the campus was so clean, and no one would've thought that behind the scenery, the beauty, the beautification...the campus was a torture chamber. Tell me what was behind that beautiful campus?

Johnny: Coming in at that time, you know...they had tall pine trees on both sides and the administration building I guess thats what you would call it, it was located be on the white side where they signed us in, then they took us on the black side, what you call the 'north campus' and that where our hell really began, they would assign you to a cottage. I was put in a cottage, they called Robinson cottage, it was the smallest cottage up there, and I was assigned to a farm crew, which went back three miles away from the cottages.

Johnny: Like I said," no one would believe us."

Antoinette: You said three miles away you was assigned to, what type of crew?

Johnny: Farm crew.

Antoinette: When you was assigned to the farm crew is that where the living hell began?

Johnny: Yes ma'am because we was working in a swamp areas, we had to go in the swamp and clean out and cut down trees to make room to plant corn and we planted corn, peas, and beans, whatever they needed planted we had to clear the ground. It was nothing but swamp area when we went there, but when we got through with it we was planting corn and stuff on it, they called it new ground.

Antoinette: I want to go back to what your day started like early in the morning and what your day end up at night. What was your day like from morning to night?

Johnny: Well we got up in the morning round about six o'clock in the morning, a guy goes and blows a bugle, we had to get up when we heard the bugle bull horn, we had to get up and put our hospitals tucks in our bed, flip our mattress, down and shower and be on line and go to the cafeteria and have breakfast, and then go to work.

Antoinette: And when you returned from work, when you come home in the evening to your cottage, what was that like?

Johnny: Well when we came back to the cottage we had to go in and do whatever Mr. Stevenson needed...or the cottage father needed us to do, clean up around the cottage or something like that and get our clothes ready for school or work the next day, our shoes had to be shine every day, and when we had a few extra minutes he allowed us to watch TV.

Antoinette: Were there any other recreational activities?

Johnny: Well that all depends on what rank my rank was. If we had, I guess, grub, rookie, explorer, pioneer, power, and ace...we had six ranks, if you had a lower rank like a grub...grub is the lowest rank was up there, you couldn't watch TV, all you could do is go to work or to school and come back, and sit in a corner, they punish you that way.

Antoinette: When I think about a living hell, and of course I haven't...I can only think about what has been described to me as 'hell', but of course a living hell is a little bit farther than what my mind can probably imagine, people being tortured, murdered, abused and horrible conditions...that's what I think about, or that's what my thoughts lead me to.

Johnny: Well that's how it was worse...it was worse than that because we was always scared because they had a vehicle we call the "Blue Goose", and when they see that Blue Goose coming round on your job or at your cottage you got scared to death because you didn't know what...whose name calling or who they was coming to pick up.

When they came to pick you up you had to ride to the white house.

Antoinette: Were you frightened?

Johnny: All the time.

Antoinette: When that Blue Goose pick you up...what was the Blue Goose? Was it was a station wagon or a police vehicle?

Johnny: It was a Ford...it was like a '57 Ford.

Antoinette: How many people was in the Blue Goose?

Johnny: They would take three boys at one time.

Antoinette: Okay, they would pick up three children ...how many men was it that picked up the boys?

Johnny: Two.

Antoinette: When they came to pick you up, where was they taking you to?

Johnny: They was taking us to the white house and they took us one at a time in the back room, we had to always wear our shirt in our pants and they would tell you to take your shirt out your pants, unbutton your pants and lay on the bed, you had to lay on your stomach, and when you lay on your stomach he had a notch in the wall that we had to look at. He said "Grab that rail...", it was a single bed with a rail like a headboard, but it was a rail and we had to hold, and he told them "If you don't...if you don't...if you turn that bed over, there's a probablity

I can kill you because I can hit you in your testicles and it might kill you, so you better hold that bed."

So he hit me the first time and I jumped up, and he slapped me upside my ear with the belt and said "nigger you get back down there, I'm going to kill you." I'm scared to death, I ain't never been hit like that in my life, so I got back down on the bed and he began to hit me and I flinch, and I can feel my body...my flesh coming off of my body through my pants every time he hit me, he had holes in this belt...in the belt too...when I got up I saw it was about three to four foot long, but it had holes in it, and when he hit me he sucked the skin from my body and I couldn't even get up off the bed, he had to come and help me get off the bed, and I was so bloody my behind was full of blood and he kept telling me that you did good...you did good..."I didn't have to kill you", he called the other boy in there and the boy was screaming and hollering and I notice that he didn't come back with us to the cottage. Me and another boy went back but the other boy doing all the screaming... they told us "He's hard, we going have to ship him to the Okeechobee campus cause we couldn't handle him like that..."

So I don't know what to think they *killed* that boy cause the way he was screaming and they was hitting him, both of them was beating him up, and he was bleeding and that added fear in me, I didn't ever want to go in that place again.

24

I had about thirty-five licks, when you get past five or six licks your behind is so numb you really can't hardly feel the rest of your body because you're numb, if we was having lunch I had to go to the cafeteria and I had to sit down ...with a pillow on my behind I was bloody, I thought he was going take me to the doctor, he said "No, I want you to go in there just like that and show them boys that we aren't playing in this place."

And that was embarrassing, all the boys kept asking "did you hold the bed?" They know that if you turn that bed a lose, you was going to be beat to death so you had to hold it. They was talking to you like you was an animal, nobody should be treated like that...

Antoinette: How many men was in the room?

Johnny: Say that again Ms. Harrell.

Antoinette: How many men was in the room?

Johnny: How many men was in the room?

Antoinette: Yes.

Johnny: It was two men. It was only one back there while he was spanking and another one if the boy was turning on the bed he would go back there and hold the boy down, and the other two boys sit out in the waiting area whatever you call it, waiting til their turn comes. Those boys was trembling with fear.

Antoinette: Was it two white men, two black men, or one white and one black?

Johnny: Oh..one was a white man, Mr. Tidwell and Mr. Marvin...Mr. Marvin was a big black man.

Antoinette: Did you say one black man and one white man?

Johnny: Yes ma'am. The black man talked to you worse than the white man did.

Antoinette: Did the black man hold you down?

Johnny: No, I held myself down cause he was hitting me on the side of my head and cross my face, he said he'll kill me, so I had to hold that bed, I didn't want to die so I had to hold the bed.

Antoinette: Was the blood coming from your body, was it coming from ...your rear end, or your legs ...was the skin busted open that required you to receive stitches from the lashes or beating?

Johnny: No...my behind was bleeding, sore and numb, my back was hit pretty bad but...all the skin came off my behind and my legs cause that's mostly were they hit me on your bottom, my butt.

Antoinette: Was your clothes soaked from the blood?

Johnny: Yes, see he told me if I turn over he was going to hit me between my balls and kill me, so that scared me right there so that's why I didn't want to turn over.

Antoinette: You held the bed as tight as you could?

Johnny: I had to hold that bed, if I didn't hold the bed he was just going to continue hitting me, he'd told me that before he even get started. "If you turn that bed a lose, I start counting all over, I'm going start all over".

Antoinette: How many times did you go to Dozier Reform School?

Johnny: I went once and I was there five years.

Antoinette: How many times did you take a ride to the White House?

Johnny: I think I went to the White House four times in the five years.

Antoinette: Was the beatings the same or did they get worse each time?

Johnny: Well, for fighting, they had a rank that was the lowest rank on the camp, was the grub, and every time you get a...a write-up you had to ride, get a ride to the white house. Sometimes if he was about the last one, he was a little lenient ...cause they was tired of beating the other ...boy.

Antoinette: What number was you placed in during the beatings? "Let's say for example if you was boy number three and it was the same two people, they was exhausted from beating the first two boys, was your beating as severe?"

Johnny: Right.

Antoinette: Did they ever change out the two men who was doing the beatings?

Johnny: Yes, they changed...they changed them. They'll be talking, they be saying "I bet you that I can make that boy bleed..", you know, they'll be talking bout "*I'll make him bleed with the first lick,*" and if he hit you straight with the belt you are hurting, but when he'd turn that belt...that belt,...like side ways and hit you, you're to going bleed on the first lick, they'll say to you get off that bed and they're betting how they make you bleed.

Antoinette: You just said they would bet on those beatings, "they made bets as in gambling..." Did you ever see money exchange hands when they made the bets?

Johnny: I didn't... ever see any money.

Antoinette: Hmm hmm,

Johnny: But you know, you didn't want to see nothing, no way, what those men was doing. You didn't want to die.

Antoinette: I want to, if I could, change the topic a little bit because something I recall, listening to a previous interview. If the boys ran away and was caught by the dogs, was there such a thing as kissing the dog's rear end?

Johnny: The boys had to kiss the private parts of the dog, that was a reward to the dog for catching him.

Antoinette: Would you talk about that?

Johnny: Yeah. what happened, we had run-a-ways and the boys, I think...I heard later they was getting dogs from the prison to run those boys down. A boy was beat so bad, I don't know whether he died or what happened to him but he had to leave the cottage, we were talking, he said he had to..."he had to kiss that dog private parts..." it was a old man ...black man that turned him in cause....the place was mostly old black people living around the school and he said the man didn't want to turn him in but he said if he didn't turn him in they would kill the people family, and so they didn't go get those boys... he say he ain't going in no swamp, the dog was eating him up, he'd be all messed up. He had dog bites all over his body and he couldn't run anymore...they brought him back and told him to take a shower, that boy was in that shower hollering with the flesh wound from the dog bites. Then couple of weeks later they had to ship that boy somewhere, they ....never told you where they're going, a lot of them would tell you they're going home, we know those boys didn't go home. Some of those boys was killed.

Antoinette: Did you ever try to run away?

Johnny: Who me?

Antoinette: Yes.

Johnny: No ma'am, I wouldn't even know what direction to go home. I never left home and you never... you was asking me the question about how it affect my mind. You know I can't...I can't really read anything, I can see a word and kind of understand it, and I never could write anything down, you know spell it out, I never could do that because the house master say he was preparing...preparing me for prison, so I didn't really need to know...really need to know anything. I say "You preparing me for prison?" He say "yeah, everybody come here after they leave here they go to prison, go home and mess up, and they go and lie on people...lie..." They say we was lying on them people up there.

Antoinette: Did you actually believe that you was going to go to prison since that's what he said that he was preparing you for?

Johnny: Well...I was...I knew I wasn't going, I was already in prison far as I was concerned, that was my prison right there. I was in a living hell right there, I didn't need to go no other place.

Antoinette: Hmm hmm. Did you really think that you were going to a school? Did you feel that you was going to a reform school that was a living hell on earth?

Johnny: Well they told us that...we was just going be away six months and that was what the police had told me, he said "I take quite a few boys from Dade City, out there.

Six months and you can come on back home. That's a good school, they'll teach you a lot up there." Well that musta wasn't on the side I was on cause, they wasn't teaching us nothing.

Antoinette: Hmm hmm...

Johnny: People don't know how cruel those people were, those people...I tell you, like I said "I had to blank a lot of that stuff out of my mind, it was God that brought me out of that hell hole. "Thats why, I blank that stuff outta my head just to survive."Those people was so...they was that mean, they was just mean. They didn't care, they treated us like we was animals, I mean we had to look at the floor and look down when we address them "yes sir...yes ma'am...no ma'am...", we couldn't look them in the face. They kept us in the swamp, they didn't care whether it cold or hot. ...you can feel the beat of your heart when you was in the swamp water, but sometimes we had to get in there when it was cold and hot. Snakes was in that water. And those boys, the little boys, I guess you might have heard of ...when it cold like that and you get in wet you get frost bitten and the boys hands, they'll be warming their hand, they didn't know if it got too warm it would be painful and I tried to help them, "Now don't get too close to the fire when you're cold like that." You can hurt yourself and be in more pain. Those boys would be crying.

they would let me kind of help them out the little boys and I was a little boy too but I was a little bigger than they were."

Antoinette: Hmmm hmm. What else would you want anyone to know about the living-hell experience?

Johnny: I experience being beat, raped, called nigger, I saw human remain in the hog pen.

Antoinette: I've heard people say that they died and came back and they saw a glimpse of heaven. I've heard people say they...drew a parallel of things that they saw some parts of hell and I'm hearing you describe to me that Dozier Reform School was as 'a living hell'.

Johnny: That's what it was, it was living hell.

Antoinette: As a child, an innocent child...having your innocence taken away from you through some hellish acts when you should have been playing in one of them beautiful theme parks in the sunshine State of Florida, but you was going through living hell. Pain and a living hell inside of a school or Dr. Souza soup medical experiments. Or recalling the yelling, the screaming, the crying of children, little boys at Dozier.

Johnny: Well they hollered all night, you know and our cottage father he was a pretty strict guy, and when he mentioned white house that kind of got the hollering up and we definitely didn't want to go there, or when we were out in the field sometime those boys just be crying, want to go see their mama or "wanna go see their daddy," *"Why these people doing us this way?"* you know I cried a lot for them kids, I cried for myself too."

Antoinette: Hmm?

Johnny: Yes, I cried too.

Johnny: We wanted to go see our mama and family.

Antoinette: So its a difference between crying for their family than crying because of what was being done to them.

Johnny: I think Ms. Harrell, it was a little of both because a lot of them are like me and never left home and never experienced the abuse that we was going through, why were we treated so bad, I mean and ...and to this day I sit here and watch the cartoon and I go to crying, I just...the sad part of it I go to crying, I'm still crying...50 years later I'm still crying for those boys, those kids, still flashings in my head. I see something sad I cry. I cried so many nights and days ...for myself and the others because I worked double hard to keep those boys from getting a ride to the white house. And I talked to a lot of them because "You got to work man, and you got to keep your mouth closed cause if you don't they are going to kill you". They said a lot of those boys went home, I don't know, I can't prove they didn't go home but I knew they hadn't earned enough rank to be going home,

I know they got a spanking a couple days go, and now they are going home.

Antoinette: What do you think happened to them?...and let me just say this, Dr Erin Kimmerle, the anthropologist from USF...is exhuming the bodies at Arthur G. Dozier Reform School. I just read about...the coffin that was exhumed with the missing body....what about the missing body? We also heard about the sweat box, what do you think happened ...when they found the coffin with the missing body, what do you think happened to some of these children?

Johnny: They could have whipped them and threw them in the pit or fed them to the hogs. But I'm just curious Ms. Harrell, because we had a cemetery called boot hill on the black side and...those bodies they found, what they're talking about is white boys, and in my mind, to this day, I know that some of those boys were killed. On my way from the job... coming from the farm we use to go cross this little old bridge and the boys use to tease me by saying "Hey Johnny, you'd be surprised how many of those little boys are buried in them little old holes right there." And I told the lady who was up there digging, I say "there's a little bridge up there..."

Antoinette: Is that Dr. Erin Kimmerle, who you told that too?

Johnny: I told her, yes.

Antoinette: Yes, hmm hmm.

Johnny: I was telling them about the saw mill and the hog pen. I said "We never had a hog on the ground, all our hogs was on concrete", Dr. Kimmerle assistant said, "yeah, I seen all that, but I didn't... know what it was." I said, "It was a concrete hog pen", and there was a little...like a bridge we use to cross, and they had like a little cemetery that me and the boys use to cross over...we ain't never seen no funeral ... they said when a person died, they ship them home.

Antoinette: So... they said that the boys was shipped home after they died, no matter what happened to them, they shipped them home. Is that what you are saying?

Johnny: If the parents didn't come for them, they'd bury them on the campus, but I never seen a hearse and no funeral or nothing like that. You'd think if a boy died there they would've had some kind of a funeral....you know, you just see a graveside, but you never seen a funeral.

Antoinette: Hmm, hmm. Okay, well if I think of anything else I need to ask you...I'll call you if thats okay with you.

Johnny: Okay, that would be fine and if I can think of anything else to tell you, I'll call you.

CHAPTER THREE

CHILD LABOR AT DOZIER

I guess they call it a frost-bite, some of the boys got their hands frost-bitten and they put it round a fire, they didn't know you couldn't get your hand warmed up as it really pained, and the boys' hands got frost-bitten and they'd be in severe pain but they had to continue to work and they couldn't even hold anything.

Antoinette: Johnny lets talk about the labor you performed at the reform School as a child at Arthur G. Dozier Reform School in Mariana, Florida?

Johnny: Well when I got there I was assigned...I was assigned to the farm crew and my crew's instructor was man named Mr. Stevenson, a black man. I was in Robinson cottage up there cause I was 11, cause he was the crew instructor and he would take us out in the swamp, we had to clear out new ground to plant corn and we had to wade in water and drop those trees cut down trees where they could haul them out on a trailer to the saw mill, the little boy there was helping me he was so small, we were pushing and pulling a two hand saw, I was pulling him, he didn't have strength enough...pulling us all back through so I was pushing and pulling, he'd beg me not to tell because if he didn't do the job, they was going to give him a spanking, so I didn't tell Mr. Stevenson about it. I was doing all the work cause he was so little he couldn't hardly stand up in that water let alone pull that throttle...and when I got a little bit bigger they put me on ...on a tractor, that was when I use to go around to different fields and pick up the corn, it'd be egg, corn and beans. I'll take it to the barn, Mr. Stevenson started me going around the cottages and picking up trash, taking it to the pit, and I had to go pick up the hog slop, me and a boy named Shazor drove a tractor and...

Antoinette: What was his name again? Would you repeat his name again?

Johnny: Shazor...I don't know his last name, his first name was Shazor, he was in Lee Cottage, he's was bigger boy and older than I was...

Antoinette: Hmm hmm, go ahead.

Johnny: We got up about 6:00 a.m...we got up in the morning by a bugle, and I mentioned Doctor Souza soup well I only took that if we had even and odd days, the even days we went to work, the odd days we went to school...

Antoinette: Okay...let's...I want to keep it on the child labor.

Johnny: Oh, okay.

Antoinette:...yeah, tell me...I really want you to go back in that time and period, I want you to go as far back as you possibly could, and I know it may jog some terrible memories, it may even go into some painful memories about the horrible days at work as a child, how long, how short those days were and how hard those days were. Tell me and anyone that is reading your book about those days.

Johnny: Well we got up at 6:00 a.m. in the morning it depend on the job that had to be done, sometimes it could be earlier than 6:00 a.m. and the barn wasn't too far from my own cottage, we had to walk to the barn and that's where we got on the tractors to go dig our field, whatever Mr. Stevenson had us working on that day.

And the weather would be so cold, it'd be so cold that...I guess they call it a frost-bite, some of the boys got their hands frost-bitten and they put it round a fire, they didn't know you couldn't get your hand warmed up as it really pained, the boys' hands got frost-bitten and they'd be in severe pain but they had to continue to work, they couldn't even hold anything in their hands cause it'd be so cold, if we didn't do the work, we would get a ride to the white house, and he would write us up. We was pulling corn and cutting cane, we were so short and the cane was so tall, the limbs on the sugarcane stalk was like razor blades and it would cut the little boys so bad. I was kind of use to it working in the fields so I helped the little boys out. I was a little boy too but I know if they didn't do their job they was going to get a spanking so I didn't want that to happen, so I was trying to help them out and that was one of the reason that Mr. Stevenson appointed me to be a driver because I was looking out for those boys and I got a spanking because one of the boys said I busted the tires on the tractor, that was my first time I had to ride to the white house, and when I got to the white house he had both of us, me and the boy named Shazor, he drove both of us because ...I told them that I didn't do it and I didn't tell that Shazor busted the tires.

Antoinette: Now...can I ask you one question here?

Johnny: Yeah.

Antoinette: When you worked in the swamps? What did you do? Please...give me details about the environment that you had to work in, in the summertime as well as winter... what was it like during the wintertime, what was it like on a average day for a child working in the summertime.

Johnny: It was cold, and we...we was out in the open, we made a fire early in the morning but the fire didn't last long, we had to go out there and work. If we was picking peas we had pick the peas, then he would take us to another field, if they had corn to get that day, we had to pull the corn, if we had sugarcane, those boys was so little, and I was too, we couldn't even reach the corn... he wouldn't give us a knife so we had to break the corn, they called it "shub the corn", a boy that wasn't even eight years old, he couldn't reach up on the top to get the corn, we had to pull it down and... carried it, the air would be so cold, and I saw that boy's hands freezing up and I walk him around the fire so he could warm his hands, warming your hand is still bad, don't stand there and continue .

to get your hand warmed because it's like a burning inside that you can't hardly stand." Some of the boys got frost-bitten, some of the boys got legs broke hauling the logs we had to haul too the saw mill, and they'd take those boys to the ... doctor and they'll just send them right back out there with a cast on their arm. It was...it was scary...scary all the time because you didn't know whether a snake was going to bite you or what... I was always scared...

Antoinette: What about the mosquitoes?

Johnny: Yes it was...we didn't pay them any attention...you couldn't pay them no mind because you had a job to do, and you didn't want to ride, when I say 'ride' that mean, they'd take you to the white house, or you did whatever you had to do, always scared. They had one car that they would put the boys in, they had a Ford, I call it 'Blue Goose', when they came round there they didn't care how little you was, if they tell you go in that swamp, you just had to go in that swamp, and I went in the swamp, the water was over my head, I was tying ropes on logs and I was trying to pull them out, and I knew snakes was out there, I seen snakes, but that didn't stop them. Mr. Stevenson told me to do that and I had to do that and no questions asked. But we was... always scared, I was always scared...they worked me like a slave. I didn't understand then, now as I look back it was slavery.

Johnny: I was 11, we had some boys in the cottage as young as seven and eight years old.

Antoinette: What year are we talking about during this time?

Johnny: 1957.

Antoinette: 1957.

Johnny: Yes, 1957.

Antoinette: Would you tell me about the type of clothing and shoes that you had on during the summer and winter?

Johnny: Well we had... uniform type pants and boots which you had to have your shoes shine, your shoes...your work shoes had to be shine, you couldn't have a button missing off your shirt, you had to sew your own clothes, if you had a tear on your clothes you had to sew it, you had a button missing you had to put it on and our clothes went to the laundry. We had school clothes and work clothes. The pants was pretty heavy ...

Antoinette: Was you ever hurt at any time while cutting the logs or the timber or did you ever see any other child hurt?

Johnny: Yeah, I seen a lot of boys break their arms and legs. I got a lot of my fingers caught in there, but it just didn't break. I got a lot of bruises on my side,

Antoinette: You just kept on working?

Johnny: Yes...

but you can't complain about that, you had to put a band-aid on it and they told you go on back to work...

Antoinette: How did the boy leg break, can you tell me about that?

Johnny: What, break?

Antoinette: Yeah, how did they break his leg? How, do you know?

Johnny: Oh, if I was pulling a log out of the swamp, he had to pull the log out the swamp, and if he got his leg in between and I couldn't see it, and I kept moving...once you get a start trying to pull a log, you don't stop, if it break his leg, he'd just take him to the hospital and bandage him up, cause they'll tell you he didn't have no business with his leg in the way..., but we were children. Like me I ain't never left my home in my life, I ain't never done these hard kind of work in my life and, like I said, you'll be scared all the time and if he told you to move that tractor you better be moving that tractor and no question asked. If a boy got his leg broke, he just got his leg broke. That was the kind of people they was, they're cruel.

Antoinette: Did they immediately come and get the little boy or did they wait or was someone on the scene such as a overseer who took them to the hospital?

Johnny: They'd call and have somebody to come take them to the infirmary.

Antoinette: Would it be immediately or would it be that they had to wait?

Johnny: If he was doing something, he'd just have to hurt, if it wasn't a life and death situation, he just hurting til somebody come and get him. Sometime they would send him back to the cottage and sometime they'd bring him back to the field.

Antoinette: Can you ever recall if any of the boys..... got bit by snakes or anything like that? Do you ever recall?

Johnny: There were a couple of boys that was with me and a snake bit them, but Mr. Stevenson knew how to make it bleed so he was pretty good at bringing up poison from a snake bite, but it hit him right there on the hand mostly when they putting their hand down in the swamp water. They had a lot of snakes up there and they was deadly poison, and they had a lot of snake that wasn't poison, but they'd bite you anyway. But he knew how to handle the poison til somebody come up there and take you to the infirmary.

Antoinette: Was there an overseer, a person who was supervising, such as a supervisor?

Johnny: Well to tell you the truth... he was a black man, he was the only man over...over the farm crew.

All the men that was over the black boys was black. The white men was over the white boys. A black man couldn't spank a white boy, but a white man can spank a black boy in 1957 when I was there.

Antoinette: How many boys would you say was working on that crew that you can remember...on any given morning?

Johnny: Roughly it was about 20 on our crew. You had boys come on different day, so you had odd and even days. Some boys went to school while other boys worked and worked while other boys went to school, so it was always somebody in the field.

Antoinette: You said you alternated between school and work?

Johnny: Right, they called it odd and even days.

Antoinette: Was there trucks taking the timber away from the swamps?

Johnny: Well we haul...we hauled the logs to the saw mill on the tractor... they had a big saw mill with a big blade on it and they used to put it up on the ramp, we could take about 10 or 15 trees at the...end of a day, we was making four by fours and two by sixes, and two by eighth pines out of them.

Antoinette: Was there...outside companies coming to pick up the timber?

Johnny: It was always trucks...at that time I don't know

...we was just trying to concentrate to keep from getting killed...but we saw trucks all the time coming in there for food and picking up vegetable, lots of trucks was there all the time.

Antoinette: Logging and cutting timber wasn't the only job you did. Did you do any other work?

Johnny: Yes, I worked on farm.

Antoinette: Hmm hmm... you just cut the timber?

Johnny: That all I did was that until I left from out there, drove tractor, worked in the field.

Antoinette: Can you recall the name of the swamp that you was cutting the timber from?

Johnny: What's that?

Antoinette: Can you recall the location of the swamp where you was cutting the timber out of?

Johnny: It was a swamp...

Antoinette: Okay.

Johnny: No, I can't remember the swamp.

Antoinette: Okay, hmm hmm.

Johnny: I was a little boy. I remember him telling me "Johnny, we going to plant some corn out there in three months", and this man pointed out to the swamp! I was... I mean I told the boys "That man is crazy!" But in three months we was picking up corn out of that place, and we had to go in that swamp and cut those trees down and drain that water out of there...

take that stuff to the saw mills and sure enough that corn was coming up out of there, he had cleared it all.

Antoinette: Was there any money that you ever received for your labor?

Johnny: No ma'am...no ma'am, I didn't get no money for no labor... we didn't even get a thank you...you better not ask them for no money.

Antoinette: Did your mother know that you was doing that kind of work, or anybody in the family know that you was being used to work in the swamp?

Johnny: No, my mother thought that I was doing alright, and when I got out of there she said "They told her they were rehabilitating me and I was doing good..." and I wasn't...they wouldn't allow my mama to come up and see me, they told her she'd a mess up the program they had for me. So my mother never did come. We had a canteen up there and they use to send money and that's where we got our cans and stuff out of the canteen.

Antoinette: Do you remember, or can you recall any of the children crying or did you cry from all the hard work...

Johnny: I always cried.

Antoinette: Oh you cried.

Johnny: Well most of my crying was...I was thinking why

was I in this place and why was I treated like...like I'm worse then animal and not going to school...we cried a lot, but we wasn't allowed to cry.

Antoinette: Did you go to work from morning to night, and if you left in the morning, did you come back...return back to your cottage in the day or was it late in the evening or was it nightfall?

Johnny: Well they fix our lunch so we...I think if I'm not mistaken Ms. Harrell, we went to the cafeteria for lunch but we had to go back to work and we got up at five.

Antoinette: Hmm hmm, you all knocked off at five o'clock?

Johnny: Yes ma'am.

Antoinette: Hmm hmm. When you knocked off that day, was the next day was a school day?

Johnny: Yes, that right.

Antoinette: The following day did you pick up where you left off or was it a new job or did you go back to the same job that you left off on or whatever they assigned you to?

Johnny: Like I was telling you, we was working on a place called new ground where we couldn't leave that place until that job was complete, all the trees and stuff had to be taken up, all those limbs and tree roots, whatever had to be cleared , but after I got a little age, I managed to get off that site. I believe I was in the swamp a lot of times because they send me in different location, if they had a order for some peas at the cafeteria, I would take the peas to the cafeteria, corn or eggs or whatever they...cause I had the tractor and the trailer.

Antoinette: Hmm hmm. Did you drive the tractor at thirteen?

Johnny: Yes ma'am.

Antoinette: Did they teach you to drive the tractor or is this something that you went there knowing how to do?

Johnny: Well he taught me how cause he always was telling me to pull it up while he can hook the chains and stuff on to the log...

Antoinette: And who is he?

Johnny: Mr. Stevenson ......he seen that I was pretty good so...he made me one of the driver.

Antoinette: Is that the person...the person who was overseeing you?

Johnny: Mr. Stevenson

Antoinette: Mr. Stevenson.

Johnny: Shazor was a tractor driver, he the one got me a spanking, the boy from Lee cottage

Antoinette: Hmm hmm... about how many, and I know this may be a tough question but, on a average day...work day between morning and evening. It sounds like a child labor camp to me and they were selling the timber and crop to outside companies. The state of Florida was running a child labor camp.

49

About how many logs would you say you cut...you sawed with your hand, on a average day?

Johnny: Well the trees was big, we would get about four or five big trees and we'd have to saw them and drop them and we had to put a wedge in the tree to keep the tree from falling down...or either falling on somebody and killing them so we got to know how to avoid the injuries or fatality...he would show us how to cut the tree and where it can drop, big trees drop. And then we had to dig...dig under the tree...under the root where you can get the tractor to pull it up. Well we'd get about five or six trees outta there a day, but he moved us around, he'd have us...he would have us out there for half a day and the other half of the day he have us picking peas, if he had a order for peas and stuff...that's the way they did it, if he had a order for something we would have to leave what we was doing and go get the order and fill that order up.

Antoinette: Hmm hmm, did you return back to that job or you just had to complete that order?

Johnny: Right...we had to go sometimes and pick up milk, eggs and take it to the cafeteria, sometimes they had boys that worked in the dairy, thats how we got milk to take to the cafeteria. We had to take sugar cane down to the cane mill.

Antoinette: Hmm hmm.

The cane mill, did it operate by machines or was it grinded by a a mule turning the machine in 1957?

Johnny: They had a ... I want to say a mule going around a stone that pressed that cane, go round and round in a circle and it pressed the cane, if I'm not mistaken. But I remember we was always talking about drinking the cane juice so...it was pressing the cane and made the syrup out of it.

Antoinette: Hmm hmm... did your hands have a lot of blisters?

Johnny: Yes ma'am..yeah.

Antoinette: What about your feet?

Johnny: Yeah. Well we had pretty good shoes on and heavy socks, so didn't...didn't bother your feet too much, just wet in the swamp, it was always wet.

Antoinette: Did you ever have to go to the infirmary because of injuries that you received due to the hard work?

Johnny: Well I had...I had blisters on my arm where rubbing against "the cane". When you're going through a cane mill, that... sugar cane is like a razor blade and it had cut my arm up pretty good because I had my arm full of it and ...wouldn't stop bleeding, they took me to the hospital and bandaged that up and he told me all week wear long-sleeved shirt, and I had a long-sleeved shirt on already.

You didn't...you didn't question those people, they told you to do something you just said, "yes ma'am, no ma'am".

Antoinette: If it wasn't that bad of a wound did you return back to work?

Johnny: Yes. I went back to work, they wrapped it up pretty good.

Antoinette: Yes, that was my question.

Johnny:... It two to three weeks to heal.

Antoinette: Hmm hmm, so you went back to work?

Johnny: Right.

Antoinette: Is there anything else that you want to tell me about the labor at Dozier Reform School in Mariana, Florida, also known as Florida Industrial School for Boys?

Johnny: That's pretty much covered it...

Antoinette: Okay and thank you for this interview.

Johnny: ... Oh! as a a young boy we had to get up and flip our mattress and put our hospital tucks in and we had to have our shoes shined... we had to make sure every button on our shirt was on there, our work shoes had to be shined and as good as our school shoes.

Antoinette: And although you was going in to the swamps to work..

Johnny: ...under the mud with shine shoes. Yes, Ms. Harrell.

Antoinette: Was there dogs on the scene when you worked?

Johnny: Nah.

Antoinette: Was there any dogs on the scene when you went to work?

Johnny: I didn't see any.

Antoinette: Was there any people with guns just in case somebody ran away? If one of the little boys...ran.

Johnny: They called a man...they called a man, you just had the regular people that worked there and if they had a runaway they called somebody in to go look for him.

Antoinette: Hmm hmm, but there was no one standing over you with a gun or rifle or dogs....

Johnny: No...no...no ma'am.

Antoinette: Hmm hmm.

Johnny: They had so much fear in them, they didn't have to have no gun.

Antoinette: Did you know anything about Child Labor Leases? Youth offenders tens years of age were leased to work on the turpentine farms and the phosphate mines under the vicious convict lease system in Florida.

Johnny: No. I didn't know that. Those people was cruel and could do anything to a child.

CHAPTER FOUR
BLOOD ON THEIR HANDS

Antoinette: I want to talk about the "blood on their hands." The boys that was murdered at the reform school. I want you to take us back to that time, period and place and what you saw from the very day that it happened?

Johnny: Ms. Harrell, sometime when you or any other boy got a beating, you had to walk in the cafteria with the blood on your clothes. So, I learned to keep my mouth closed when I seen stuff like that.

Antoinette: Johnny you was talking about boy foot in the pot?

Antoinette: Was the flesh on the foot or did the boys foot appear to be cooked. Did it appear that it was just put in the pot?

Johnny: It was just a foot with the flesh on it? They put it in that big pot where it was cooking with the hog slop.

Antoinette: You saw the foot, was it just the bones of the skeleton remains?

Johnny: I saw the flesh on the foot. The whole foot?

Antoinette: Was that the first time that you had seen body parts in the hog pen with your own eyes?

Johnny: Well, that is the first time I saw the foot thats right. The other boy saw it to, he witnessed seeing the foot?

Antoinette: Is there any other thing or any other incident that you can recall thats related to children being buried, human remains, anything that would be noticeable?

Johnny: I saw a boy's hand in the trash pit. I was taking trash to the trash pit. That's when I saw the boys hand. The other boy told me not too say anyhing because that could be my hand in the trash pit. When I put the trash in the pit everything would be burned.

Antoinette: Johnny did you end up going around to different pits or where there different pits?

Johnny: I went only to one pit and I went around too different cottages picking up trash.

Johnny: went to the cafeteria and pick up the food and take it to the hog pen?

Johnny: The food was already cooked, but they would cook it a second time before they gave it to the hogs.

Antoinette: The boy who told you to be quiet was that his first time seeing body parts?

Johnny: I don't know if was his first time, it was my first time. The hand and the foot was in two different locations.

Antoinette: What state of mind did this leave you in after seeing and such a thing?

Johnny: Scared to death. I knew that the people was killing the boys and that really made me scared.

Antoinette: Do you know of those boys was black or white?

Johnny: They were black, there no whites where I was. There was black boys on that side. It was all black.

Antoinette: You told me once before there was a fire pit. Right. Talk to me about that fire pit.

Johnny: That's right, I was telling you about the time when the boys was warming themselves around the fire. I am guessing that's the same thing you're talking about.

Antoinette: I remember a conversation we had about a cemetery not being very far from the fire pit?

Johnny: It was the cemetery not from the cottage. I was in Robinson cottage the same cottage. The cemetery was behind Robinson cottage.

Antoinette: Who dug the graves for the dead boys?

Johnny: I don't know.

Antoinette: You never seen anyone dig the graves?

Johnny: I never seen anyone did a graves.

Antoinette: Did any of the boys in your cottage come up missing mysteriously?

Johnny: Yes, a run- a-way. I don't think I ever mentioned that or I might have, but we had a run –a-way. There was a program put in place if your cottage didn't have a run-a-way, you could go to the beach or movie. If you had run-a-way, we had to wait until next year.

Antoinette: Did you ever hear from those boys again?

Johnny: No.

Antoinette: Johnny in the news just recently it was mentioned that nine children was found in the sweat box.

Antoinette: Have you ever heard of a sweat box when you were there or was that before your time?

Johnny: That was before my time. They didn't have anything like a sweat box that I remember. That was before me.

Antoinette: Now lets go back to the cemetery again was the name of the cemetery boot hill?

Johnny: Right and all black boys was buried in boot hill cemetery, it was segregated.

Antoinette: Boot Hill cemetery was a segregated cemetery?

Johnny: Yes!

Antoinette: Did you ever attend a funeral?

Johnny: No. I know they use to talk about it, but we never seen a funeral. We never seen the buriers.

Antoinette: Were you ever told that one of your fellow students or inmates had died?

Johnny: No

Antoinette: Were they called students in the cottage you were in?

Antoinette: How did they refer to you or the other students in the cottage with you?

Johnny: They had numbers, but they called us by our names.

Antoinette: Is that how they identified you?

Johnny: By our names.

Antoinette: The questions that I asked, if a little boy died in the cottage, did they ever tell you or inform your cottage that one of your fellow students or the inmate died?

Johnny: No

Antoinette: If a boy in the cottage died or was killed. Was a message given to you all through anyone that the little boy had died?

Johnny: No ma'am. Not at at all?

Johnny: No, stuff like that you wouldn't have known.

Johnny: Because you was not a orphanage then your mother could have been notified if something would've happened, like you passed away or mysteriously died, your family could have been notified? Yes.

Antoinette: The little boys who were orphanages of the state was they buried on the campus?

Johnny: Right. We were all part of the state.

Antoinette: Did you ever see any boys really ill and sick in your cottage?

Johnny: When we really got sick they would take us to the infirmary. I've seen quite a few boys from the White House and they was beat down pretty bad, but they didn't send them to the infirmary.

Antoinette: Did some of them ever returned back to the cottage?

Johnny: Some did and some didn't.

Antoinette: What about the ones who didn't return?

Antoinette: Did you ever hear anything from them or what happened to them?

Johnny: The boys around the cottage would say, you know, we always thought they beat those boys to death.

The cottage father stated the boys parents came by and picked him up and he went home, but we know they were lying because he didn't have no way to go home. He had to have a certain rank before he can go home.

Antoinette: Did you see blood throughout your entire time?

Johnny: Yes!

Antoinette: Did you see blood on other children?

Johnny: Some of them would get hurt on the job and they started bleeding from their injuries? Or when they was raped.

Johnny: And when they went to the White House for a beating.

Antoinette: Was you scared to go back around the hog pen?

Johnny: Yes, because I didn't know what I was going to see?

Johnny: If I didn't go, I would've made it bad for myself. I would have to explain the reason why I didn't want to go back.

Antoinette: You never told anyone?

Johnny: I didn't want to ride to the White House.

Antoinette: Did you talk to anyone about it in the cottage or did you remain silent about it?

Johnny: We sometimes talked among ourselves about it. We didn't know what had happened. But you didn't talk about it with anybody else?

Antoinette: Did you talk about it with the boys?

Johnny: Yes, at work.

Antoinette: Did it appear to be the hands of a boy under the age of 10? Or the hand and a foot of little boy over the age of 10?

Johnny: It was a little boy.

Antoinette: Was the foot sticking up out of the food for the hogs?

Johnny: Right.

Antoinette: Do you think after they cooked it the second time, they cut his body and put it into the food or do you think that the boys who was cooking the food knew that the body parts was in all the pigs food?

Johnny: They knew it was in there. All they did was just feed it to the hogs.

Johnny: They had a grinder there where they grinded the bones.

Antoinette: Do you think they were afraid to say something about it ?

Johnny: You didn't talk about nothing whatever you saw and whatever went on that place stayed in that place.

Antoinette: Did you ever tell your mother or anyone else in your family once you was released from the reform school?

Antoinette: Did you tell them what you saw in the hog pen?

Johnny: I told my brother, my cousin, and my mother too.

Antoinette: Did they believe you?

Johnny: No.

Antoinette: What do you think about all of the bodies that they are exhuming on the campus *now?*

Antoinette: Is this bringing back memories for you of the torture and the beatings as we talk about these subjects?

Johnny: Yes, it is Ms. Harrell and its hard to talk about it.

Antoinette: Why was those bodies parts all over the place like that? Do you know?

Johnny: I don't know. It where they wanted them to be. I guess they put them in different places where the bodies couldn't be found.

Antoinette: Was this black and white boys or was it black boys? My heart goes out to you and all the other men who experience this kind of hellish nightmare.

Johnny: No white boys would've been on the black side for no reason. Because the campus was segregated?

Antoinette: What was the youngest age of the children in your cottage?

Johnny: Seven years old.

 Antoinette: Did your family come and visit you?

Johnny: No

Antoinette: Do you know if any of those little children had family members to come and visit them?

Johnny: Yes, someone came and seen them and some of them even got a chance to come to the cottage with their family. They will cry to go home with their parents .

Antoinette: When you saw the hand in the hog pen, did the hand have all five fingers on it?

Johnny: Look like the hands was cut at the wrist at the joint.

Antoinette: They didn't grind it up in the machine with the other parts of the body.

Johnny: They grinded it up with the corn. They had corn and bones. They had them big old bones. They had like when they go and kill the cows and stuff.

Antoinette: Why do you think the hogs was raised on the cement versus the ground. This is my first time I've been heard something like this.

Johnny: I don't know. I didn't know, we had hogs on the ground at our home.

Antoinette: Did you ever work with any other animals or slaughtered any of the cows.

Johnny: No.

Antoinette: What age were you at that time?

Johnny: I was about 15 going on 15.

Antoinette: Were any of the little boys at 9 years old, 10 years old helping to slaughter any of the cows?

Johnny: No, they wouldn't have them messing with the cows.

Antoinette: Do you ever have nightmares about the body parts you saw in the hog pen ? At one time, I did. It has been so long now. I do have problems sleeping now.

Antoinette: Johnny it has been 50 years now. How do you feel knowing that people want to hear what you have to say about things that you saw and experience as Dozier?

Johnny: I've tried to tell my story a long time ago, people merely believe me and I know I was telling the truth. I guess we called it that we survived, I don't know. I want to thank you Ms. Harrell for helping me to tell my story. I pray for you all the time. You've done a lot to help me tell people what happened at Dozier. I have spoke at the library where I live and the people really paid attention to what I was saying.

I want to tell them how bad that place was and how I use to get up in the morning at the sound of a bugle. It was hard for people to believe that a school was treating us like that so I just quit talking about it.

Johnny: I haven't talked about it for a long time until I met you. I just wanted to talk with someone who would believe me. I talked with the White House boys.

Antoinette: Do you think they're going to find more bodies?

Johnny: Yes, Ms. Harrell, they're going to find more bodies and some they'll never find. Some of the boys were eaten by the alligators, they'll never find some of the boys.

Johnny: I don't think they're trying to find anything that happened to the black boys. Yes, they're going way back some 90 odd years ago. I told Dr. Kimmerle a lot about it and I told her about the cottage we lived in. It wasn't nothing but swamps.

Antoinette: Was the hog pen a large pen?

Johnny: Yes..

Antoinette: Really?

Johnny: Yes, they had some 15 to 16 pigs. It was a big place. We had the biggest hogs you ever wanted to see. Boy they was big.

Antoinette: What is another bloody scene or something that was horrible that took place at there?

Johnny: I saw a little boy all cut up with a a chainsaw.

Antoinette: How did that take place?

Johnny: We had a belt we put the trees up on and he was pushing it, he got to close too that saw and the boy pushed the tree and when he did he got his hand cut right off. I thought he was going to die, but they admitted him to the hospital. He was to little to use a saw-- that big pine tree was cut in half. I told him that boy was too little to be using that saw, but they wouldn't listen.

Antoinette: Are you waiting to see what the latest report will reveal from Dr. Kimmerle?

Johnny: Yes. I'm waiting to see what the latest report is going to be from Dr. Kimmerle? They can't find no black people to come forward for the DNA. The DNA is suppose to identify the body. I don't know, I hope they find a way, I hope Dr. Kimmerle would go on the black side.

Antoinette: You're going to be a guest on Vanity Fair Confidential, "Discovery Investigation" how do you feel now that your story is going to be told? You have a major opportunity to come forward to public to tell your side and I mean your account,

Johnny: Well, it was good that I got a lot of relief, but the first time I needed to go back and see the place and a couple of men and I went back to Marianna with you for the first time in over fifty years. Being on your radio and television talk show help as well. The others men may not talk about it, but it helps me to talk about it.

Antoinette: I'm happy to hear that you will be on the Vanity Fair Confidential Discovering Investigation television program to bring forth your story according to your own experiences and those little boys who died at Arthur G. Dozier Reform School.

Antoinette: Johnny the reporter said in a conservation with you, that the black guys have been silent. It hasn't been very much on the black men and for the last two years we've been working very hard at trying to get this story out. Why has there been so much silence with the media on the black man?

Johnny: I don't know, we were treated worst then the white boys. The white boys recieved a better education to.

Antoinette: Do you think the media really gave more attention to what was happening to the white men as little boys on the campus and less interested to the black men and their experience at Dozier ?

Johnny: I do, I really do because I didn't see any of them doing the hard work like the black boys did. They didn't pick beans. I think we didn't get the education and stuff like the white boys did. They had different types of jobs then the black boys had?

Antoinette: The first time that you told your story was I the first person that interviewed you and help you to take your story to the public?

Johnny: Yes ma'am it was the first.

Antoinette: Did the national and international media reached out to the White House organization?

Johnny: Right, all the black men talked about the beatings and the lashes they received?

Johnny: A lot of them don't want to even come forward and talk about it at all because they were treated so badly and they're totally embarrassed to tell their story about what happened to them. They don't want anybody to knon they were molested. Some are still afraid that something might happen to them to this very day.

CHAPTER FIVE
THE SYSTEM VIOLATED MY RIGHTS

I want to personally acknowledge Ms. Antoinette Harrell for doing a wonderful job helping us with research, advocacy, and with getting our stories told. We would never have come this far without her, and to God be the glory.

It's only God that is guiding us and leading us. What I want is for the truth to come out. We know what we saw. I know what I saw. It can't be denied. I wish it hadn't happened, but it did happen to me while I was at that school as a child. I still wonder at 67 years old, why me? I can't understand it.

I believe it was only because my mother was on welfare and she had 13 of us. Thank God I was the only brother that came to Marianna. Because of the way I was treated, I went back and told them that was *not* the place for them to go. It was pretty rough.

I don't know what the end result of the exhumations and investigation will be. I would love for what we talk about to really be found there. It is time for the truth to come out. That ground is covered with boys. I know that for a fact, I'm not going by any hearsay.

We were under a lot of threats when we went to Marianna as young boys. We worked that place. I learned – I learned a lot. One thing I surely did teach us was how to shut my mouth – because I wanted to survive. I wanted to go home.

When you're in a place that's five hours away from your home and you don't see your family members for five years, you wonder what's been happening. I wondered a lot.

They would mislead my mother with phony reports about how I was doing.

"Johnny's doing good." "He got a spanking today."

My mother had no idea that "spanking" meant my body was being practically torn in half. And when I went home and told her, she said, "No, we got good reports on you!"

It's like everything is starting all over again – we always have to be left behind. Why are we always the last to find out anything? All I know is that when things started happening on the black side of Dozier, once again we were the last to find out. We're kind of left out on everything, when *we* are the ones who worked like slaves on that side of the campus.

I'm from Dade City, Florida. I'm 67 years old now. I was imprisoned in Marianna at the Florida School for Boys for all of '57, '58, '59, and from '60 to '61. I was sent there for not going to school – for truancy.

I spent approximately five years in that place. With the help of my daughter, Catina, who I rely on for a lot of my information, I received my records from the Florida State Archives. Those records say that I was only there from January 16, 1959 to September 30, 1959. This is false information.

The records also say that I was in a glee club. I didn't even know what a glee club was! And they said I had a high rank at the school. You started as a Rookie, the next rank was Explorer, the next rank was Pioneer, the next rank was Pilot, and the highest rank on the campus was Ace.

I only remember being a Grub, zero to 1, 2, 3…it took three months to get out of the Grubs. That was the punishment rank for bad behavior, for fighting and stuff like that.

Sometimes you just had to fight to nip something in the bud. For example, we had to walk in a line, a hand's distance apart. If a guy touched you on the behind, that was a cause to fight – you got the shake. But when you fought, then you got a spanking. If the cottage father tried to stop us and we didn't stop, we both had to go to the White House.

CHAPTER SIX
FROM THE JAIL CELL TO THE
REFORM SCHOOL

I remember that when I was picked up, they said I was going to see a judge. They put me in a cell, but the judge never showed up. I kept asking when the judge was gonna come. Finally, I got my answer.

"Well, there ain't gonna be no judge. You're on your way to Marianna."

The next morning, an officer handcuffed me and put me in a car and they took me to Marianna. When we got into Marianna, he bought me a hamburger and took the handcuffs off so I could eat the burger. Then he put them back on me.

I went inside to see the director. I had to take shots and fill out papers and stuff, and then he took me on the black side. Registration was on the white side, but then I was taken to the black side. That's where I got my clothes and I was assigned to a cottage.

I was assigned to Robinson cottage, which was the smallest cottage up there. That's when my hell began.

Boys didn't spend much time in the cottages – basically we could only go in to use the bathroom, sleep, or watch TV in the TV room on weekends. Other than that, we were working – hard work and long hours.

If we had enough strength left over, we could stay on the field playing basketball until time to go to bed. Each cottage had its own play field with a basketball goal, and you could play volleyball and baseball.

I think they worked us about 8 hours a day. We didn't work any half a day. Our work and school days alternated. We worked the whole day one day, and we went to school until 2 or 3 o'clock the next day.

We got up by the bugle. In the morning, the guy would get up and blow that bugle. When the bugle blew, you had to be up, flip that mattress, put that hospital tuck in the sheets, and in five or six minutes you had to be on line, dressed to go to work.

I worked on the farm crew when I was just 11 years old. I liked to hunt anyway. When I got there, they put me on the tractor crew. Mr. Shazer said I was easy to teach how to drive a tractor, so I didn't have any 70 problem with the hook and log going through the swamp.

We cleared the ground in a lot of places. I wasn't afraid of snakes and alligators and everything, so I'd go out there and hook the logs and stuff. Since I wasn't afraid of that, he made me a tractor driver.

The guys that I worked with were friends, but they were in different cottages. I was friends with some of the guys in my cottage. You didn't get to be close friends with anyone. We weren't allowed to. I didn't have any guys there from my hometown. Most of the guys had some from their home town, but I didn't have any from Dade City. So I more or less hung out by myself.

I'd go around and clean up the garbage from different cottages. I went to different areas in the pits, and that's where I saw a boy's hand – in the pit.

We had a sawmill there, where we made all the 4x4's and 2x6's. I saw that hand in the area of the sawmill. I told another boy what I saw.

"Hey man, that looks just like a hand!"

"Johnny, don't you ever say that again," he said. "*Your* hand will be out in this pit if you ever mention that to *anybody*."

I was pretty scared then, sure enough. The same thing happened when I was picking up the slop. The hogs they had, I never saw a hog on the ground. All the hogs that we had were on concrete. I saw a boy staring at something in the pot where they cooked all the food. Then I saw what it was.

"Man, that looks like a body part! Looks like everywhere I go, I'm seein' dead people!"

He said, "You think them chil'ren is being cooked?"

"Look in the pot right there," I said. "Man, they cookin' these boys!"

At night when they had a runaway, when I asked what happened to the guy, the answer would be that he got sent home. But we knew…

This one tractor was kind of stationary. It could be moved around because they had the big saw and they had the board that we used to push the log up on and push it down into the saw. It was kind of in the pig area, right by the swamp.

When we were there, we had the tractor barns that kept our tractor.

They had two of those big grain silos. And there was something else. It was pretty watery where that sawmill was. I remember that because the guys used to have to go out there and cut the logs in the winter months.

The hog pens were concrete, I remember that. I never saw a hog on the ground. They had the prettiest hog you ever saw in your life. It was big.

We had our own bull and we had our own cows. This was the first place I ever saw a cow cross-bred with a needle. And the dairy calf came out beautiful. So it worked – they didn't ever have to have a bull to get a calf. They could just insert the needle!

The dairy was a big old place, too. So much land! Richard and I were talking when we visited the campus. We hadn't been in that place in 50 years, and God is our witness, we didn't know we were that close to town when we were there as young boys.

I saw in the paper that over 2,000 gallons of milk were collected a day at FSB! Over a thousand dozen eggs were gathered!

All the years I stayed at FSB, I did not know we were so close to town. We had the impression in our heads that town was a long way off. Now all these years later, when we visited the campus and then we went to town, I said, "Oh my God, we were right in town!"

They didn't want us to know that, no sir! See, those dog boys didn't play. They didn't want us to know how close to town we were when we were there.

The work we did was hard. I learned to deal with pain. If we were hurt, we couldn't complain about it.

Lifting, you hurt your back but you really couldn't complain about it.

They had a psychiatrist who used to give us a soup to take; said it would help our minds to keep us from thinking crazy stuff. I don't think it helped me at all. I think I just took it to keep from getting beaten to death. I think Ms. Harrell found out that this guy wasn't even licensed to give us medicine. You blank a lot of that stuff out of your mind to survive.

Ms. Harrell told us that a judge was sentenced for selling children into a for-profit prison. A Pennylviania judge was convicted for selling children into a prison for cash. Sixty-one years old Mark Ciavarella Jr., was sentenced to thirty years for making money for under the table deals with developers. He sentenced thousands of children and adults, some children as young as ten year old. Ciavarella made more than a millon dollars selling people into the penal system.

CHAPTER SEVEN
BLOODY AND DEADLY BEATINGS

Beatings were very common at the White House. We couldn't call them beatings. We had to call them spankings so no one would guess how brutal, even sometimes deadly, they were.

I know for a fact that some of the boys that they said went home hadn't been at FSB long enough to be going home. They hadn't served the program. And if they were a runaway they said, "Well, we had to send him to another location," they had the dog boys go out and run them down with the dogs.

When they would catch a runaway boy, they'd make him kiss the dog's private part, like a reward for the dog. And when the dogs got through with them, we saw the trademark on the boys that the dogs caught up with. Those guys would be torn half in two when they came back to the cottage. So if they didn't come back, we know something.

We never saw a gravesite, though. We never saw a funeral. If they buried those boys, it was something that we didn't see.

A blue Ford would drive by the cottage and we would shake from fear of going to the White House. It was terrible. One time I got a "spanking" because of a guy trying to get out of working.

"Let's bust the trailer tires so we won't have to work today," he said. "I'm not gonna do that," I told him.

He went ahead and busted the tires, and told the crew leader that I did it. I got taken over to the White House. Man, Mr. Marvin Marbely was about 6 feet tall and weighed about 300 pounds, and there was little old me lying on this bed getting spanked by him.

You had to get on the bed on your stomach and you had to grab the railing. They had a little notch on the wall and you had to lie there and look at that notch, and you had to hold onto that bed.

Mr. Marbely had two belts. One of them had holes in it. When he hit you with that belt, when he came up off it, it drew the skin off your body. He hit me so hard that I turned the bed loose, and then he hit me right upside the head with that belt. Man, I didn't know *what* to do. The next thing he said to me scared me to death.

"You know, boy, if you don't lay back down there, I'm 'on kill you."

I didn't know *what* to do. There was nobody I could tell. I had to lay there and I had to take those licks. So I laid there and I took 'em.

We all called it "spanking" because they didn't say "whooping" or "beating" – we had to say "spanking." If I told my mama I got a spanking that day, she had no idea I was half *dead*.

After the spanking, you had to take a pillow into the cafeteria with all these boys. Your behind would be bloody like a dog, and you had to go in there. Any time somebody took a "ride" to the White House and we see him with a pillow, we all want to know one thing.

"Did you hold that bed?" That's all they want to ask you. And quite naturally, you're

81

going to lie that you did, because you don't want to be a sissy. "Yeah, I held the bed," I lied.

No, I didn't hold that bed. Man I turned that thing loose, but when I jumped up and I looked up at that big old man, I knew I'd better get back down on that bed!

They were crazy people! They had no heart for children, no compassion for children. Any time a guy would beat you so bloody and then tell you to go to the cafeteria bloodied down with all those boys sitting there, then that's to set an example.

They would turn that belt sideways and it would cut about an inch down into your behind! You'd be bleeding like a hog, and they'd be joking about it. They'd make them bleed in the first four or five licks.

They were cruel people. I often wondered, "My God, what have we done to deserve this kind of punishment? Not goin' to school?" My daughter found that the term they used on my paperwork was "incorrigible." I was sent to Marianna for incorrigible behavior and truancy.

Plenty of boys went to the hospital. And the dogs, those dogs! They'd go get those boys that ran away.

At the time we were there, if you didn't have a runaway for a year, you got a chance to go to the movies or to the Panama City Beach. If you had a runaway, they'd bring the boy back to face you.

"This is the guy that messed you all up from going out to the beach. What y'all wanna do with him?"

He had messed us up for a whole *year*, so this boy had to go through a belt line with all those boys.

He messed us up, so we had to beat him.

When he got to the end of that line, we'd about killed that boy. He'd be so bloody when he got through. These guys went *crazy*, many of the them hitting him upside the head. Then we didn't ever see that guy again. They'd say they took him home.

Johnny Lee Gaddy returns back to Dozier after 50 years.

Photo Credit: Walter C. Black, Sr.

Bottom Picture: Johnny Lee Gaddy get an interview at the site of Dozier

Johnny Lee Gaddy News Inteviews

Photo Credit: Walter C. Black, Sr.

Johnny Lee Gaddy interview at the Candlelight Vigil in Marianna, Fl.

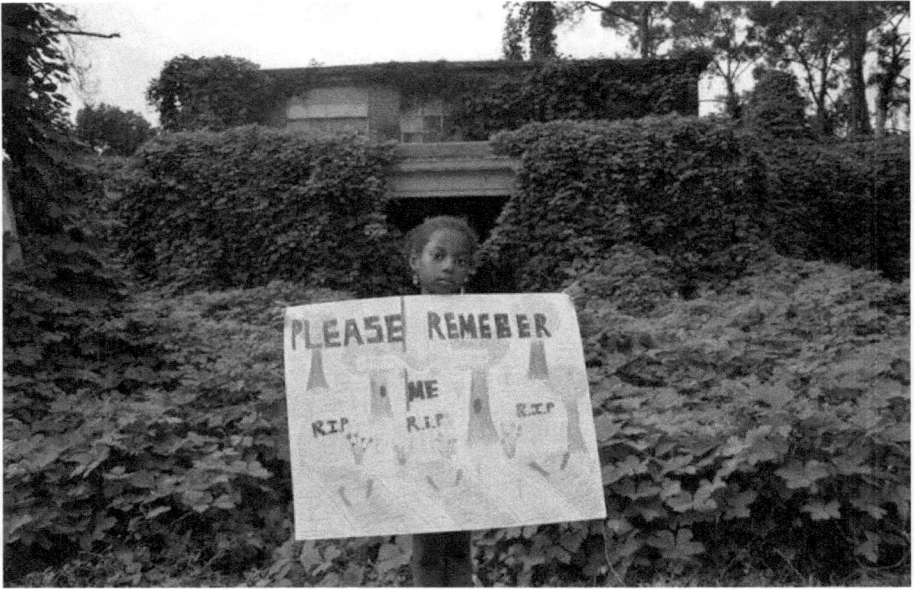

Joelle LaCoste hold artwork of Imani Blossom.

Please remember them.

Photo Credit: University of South Florida

Photo Credit: University of South Florida

Photo Credit: Walter C. Black, Sr.

Florida Cabinet in Florida. Govenor Rick Scott and
Attorney General Pam Bondi allow researcher to begin
exhuming umarked graves at the Dozier School
for boys, a now-closed notorious reform school.

Photo Credit: Walter C. Black, Sr.

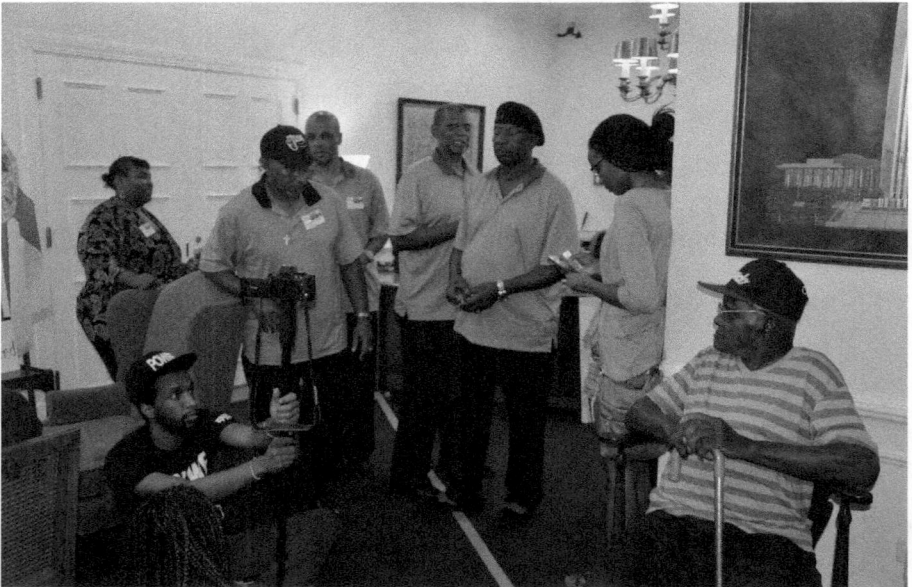

Florida Cabinet

Art Rocker (Operation People for Peace)
Photo taken at the at the hearing for the Dozier School for boys. Florida's Cabinet decided it will allow researchers to begin exhuming the unmarked graves.

CHAPTER EIGHT
DR. SOUZA SOUP EXPERIMENT

As sent to the Medical Research Department, after searches by personnel in the below contacts. Neither showed up on their records, the researcher was kind enough to go into archives and view several drawers of micofilm which takes about 1-2 hours to view based on my own viewing of microfilm here in Clearwater.

Robert Straley

Antoinette: Johnny I would like to talk about the Dr. Souza Soup medical experiment. First tell me who was Dr. Souza.

Johhny: He was suppose be a psychiatrist.

Antoinette: Why did you go to see him?

Johnny: I went to see because they said I had a nervous break down.

Antoinette: To your knowledge did you have a nervous break down?

Johnny: When I got a beating, I began withdrawn and the cottage father said he became concern. He recommend that I see Dr. Souza.

Antoinette: Johnny tell me about the first visit.

Johnny: Dr. Souza asked me what was wrong and I explained to him that I was missing home and I got a beating for something I I didn't do. I was hollered at all the time. My cottage father called me boy all the time and Tidwell called me a dumb nigger all the time. He called all the black boys a numb nigger all the time. One time he slapped me up side my head and told me, "nigger get back down on the before I killed you." Between being sexual abused and afraid that I was going to be killed this mess mind up. I opened up and told Dr. Souza what I was gone through.

Antoinette: Did you trust Dr. Souza?

Johnny: No, he didn't believe what I was saying.

He said that a lot boys came in saying the same and they didn't have proof about the things they were saying.

Antoinette: What did he tell you after you told him what you was going through?

Johnny: He told me to keep that kind of stuff to myself. He told me the soup that we was going to give was going to help me. He told me that I had to come there twice a week. He was writing what I told him down.

Johnny: Ms. Harrell, he made me take the soup in his office. He wouldn't give me any soup to take back with me to the cottage.

Antoinette: Was he a black doctor or white doctor?

Johnny: He was a white doctor?

Antoinette: Tell me about the second visit.

Johnny: He told me that he was going to give me some soup to take. He was studying and monitoring how it made me feel. He watched me for three month. He asked me if I was still withdrawn, being by myself and missing home?

Johnny: He also gave me a little white pill to take with the soup.

Antoinette: Johnny was your mother aware that you was seeing a doctor for anything?

Johnny: No, my mother wasn't aware of anything that was going. They told me that I was a ward of the state and they didn't need her permission to do anyting.

Antoinette: Were you afraid to see this doctor?

Johnny: I was afraid to see him.

94

Antoinette: Johnny, in a previous interview you told me that they put something on your head to test your brain. Tell me about that.

Johnny: He connect a lot of wires to my head to see what my brain was doing.

Antoinette: Did it shock you?

Johnny: No, it did shock me.

Antoinette: Was the doctor by himself when he performed the test?

Johnny: There was other boys from Dozier there helping him.

Antoinette: Was it black or white boys?

Johnny: It was white boys.

Antoinette: What was the white boys doing?

Johnny: They was hooking up the monitors, they had been doing that kind of work. They was recording what was on the machine to determine how much soup I had to take that day.

Johnny: I was nervous everytime I had to go and see them people.

Antoinette: What was the ages of the white boys?

Johnny: I would say about fifteen or sixteen years old.

Antoinette: Do you feel like they were experimenting on you?

Johnny: Yes, they was using us as guinea pigs.

Antoinette: I know you was very young, but did you see any medical certificates on the wall?

Johnny: I didn't pay any attention to it.

Antoinette: Johnny, did the soup make you feel any kind of way?

Johnny: I told him that it was helping me, I didn't feel anything from it. The soup had a bitter taste. I don't know what it was made out of .

Antoinette: Was it black or boys only? Or was there white boys as well?

Johnny: We was segregated, I would know.

Antoinette: Back to how it made you feel.

Johnny: The pill was making feel drowsy. It made me feel sleep. We couldn't take it when we were working. We had to take it the day we was going to school.

Antoinette: How long did you see Dr. Souza?

Johnny: I visit him for about three months and each visit was about an hour long.

Antoinette: What did you do in that one hour?

Johnny: I laid on the bed with the machine on my head.

Antoinette: Was Dr. Souza, young or elderly?

Johnny: He looked to be about fifty years old.

Antoinette: Did the other boys tell you how the soup made them feel?

Johnny: Yes, they told me how it made them feel. The other boys said that its time for us to go and take this crazy soup.

Antoinette: How many boys went to see Dr. Souza at time?

Johnny: They only take three at a time.

Antoinette: Who took you to the doctor's office?

Johnny: One of the instructor who did the whipping took us to see the doctor.

Antoinette: Johnny was it the same boys or was it different boys?

Johnny: In my cottage it was the same boys.

Antoinette: Was he the only doctor working in the office or was there others?

Johnny: He was the only one that was a psychiatrist?

Antoinette: Did any of the other boys show any signs of mental illness?

Johnny: No!

Antoinette: Describe how the soup look.

Johnny: It was an herbal soup, I didn't see any meat any the soup. It was dark brown in color with a bitter taste to it. I had to drink one bowl of soup.

Antoinette: Can you recall any of the other boys talking about Dr. Souza any kind of way?

Johnny: We really didn't want no one to know that we were on that crazy stuff, so we didn't go around talking about that stuff to anyone.

Antoinette: Did you tell your mother when you was released from Dozier?

Johnny: I told her the same things I'm you. I really didn't know how to explain that kind of stuff.

Antoinette: Did Dr. Souza have nurses working with him?

Johnny: He had a lady working sometimes. He mostly had the white boys from the school.

Antoinette: Did you have a conversation with the white boys?

Johnny: No, we did talk. They just hooked all the wires to my head, my chest and on my fingers.

Antoinette: White boys didn't have to do farm work. They got certificates for their studies. We didn't get any certificates for anything.

Antoinette: Was he mean or rude to you?

Johnny: No, he didn't hold much of a conversation with you. He didn't spend much time with you.

Johnny: Robert Straley told me that Dr. Souza didn't have license to practice medicine.

Antoinette: Johnny I found a lot of helpful information and helpful research by Robert Straley. Based on his research there are no medical licenses that can be found for either Dr. Louis Souza or Dr. Robert Loyal Currie as of May 21, 2013. Dozier School for Boys were hiring medical staff without any licenses to practice medicine in any field. Robert Straley contacted the Medical Quality Assurance Licenser Services. Robert stated that he also contacted the Medical Archives Research and (Note: that he didn't published the researcher's name of email address unless asked by a judge or court order. Robert searched different spelling variations of Louis name; Louis Souza, Luis Souza, Luis de Souza, and nothing could be found. Dr. Louis Souza and Dr. Robert Loyal Currie worked there from 1955-1965. The school was called The Dozier School for Boys, before that the Florida School for Boys and before that Florida Industrial School for Boys. The original name was the Florida Reform School.

Antoinette: You said that the soup taste like it had an herbal taste?

Johnny: Yes I did.

Antoinette: According to an article by Joy Reese Shaw in the St. Peterburg Times. The man who called himself Dr. Souza reportedly believed that behavioral disorders developed when the blood did not carry a sufficient amount of oxyen to blood cells. His soup was a mixture of concentrated protein made from red bone marrow.

Antoinette: Johnny, we can't call him Dr. Souza, let's just say Souza was conducting neurological examination, laboratory studies and electro-encephaloraph on you and the boys.

Johnny: Ms. Harrell, ain't no telling what those people was doing.

Antoinette: Johnny is there anything else you want to tell me about the medical experiment?

Johnny: No, I think I've told you everything I can remember.

CHAPTER NINE

MODERN DAY SLAVERY AT DOZIER

Dozier reform school was a child labor camp. Modern Day Slavery took place on the campus. Follow the sells from the produce, livestock, timber, poulty and it will tell you everything you need to know how this modern day slave camp for children.

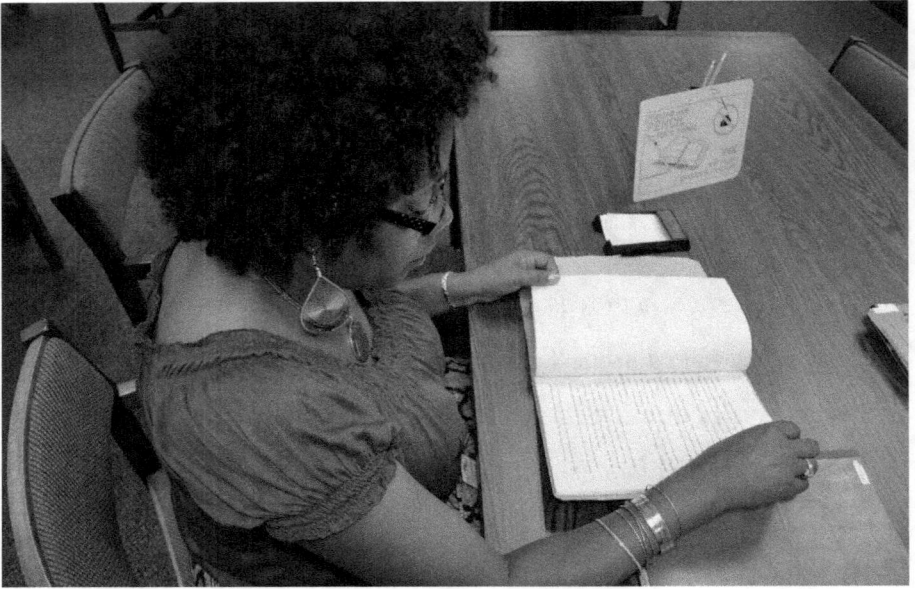
Antoinette Harrell researching at the Florida State Archives.
Photo Credit: Walter C. Black, Sr.

Johnny I believe every word that you have told me in the interview. I've researched peonage cases in sixteen states and this is one of the worse cases of child abuse and torture that I have found in my research. Often times we think of child labor in other countries. Perhaps some people in the United States want to turn a blind eye and a deaf ear to the screams of children who were victims of abuse. The boys at Dozier wasn't screaming with excitement from the theme parks. They were screaming out of fear, being torture, abuse and from being used as modern day slaves.

I sincerely hope that The Florida Department of Law Enforcement continue to conduct a fresh inquiry that will lead them to a new criminal investigation of past abuses at the now close infamous Dozier. Reform School. Your bravery will help shed some light on the dark and evil history of abuse and modern day slavery that took place at the infamous reform school. No child should experience these horrible evil acts. The men that did this to you can't be called men. They should be called demons in human formation. After interviewing you for your book. I understand why you chose the title for this book. Dozier was a living hell and when I think of a hell, I think of demons, and that what you met. Its truly a miracle that you made it out of the hell den and child labor camp alive.

In all the research that I have conducted on the subject of peonage and involuntary servitude this is by far the worst. Dozier Reform School has the appearance of a child labor camp. After interviewing several of the black men who worked on the farms, growing produce, raising livestock and poulty to be sold and slaughtered.

Dozier Reform school produced millions of dollars of produce, timbers, livestock and poultry. Child labor is against the law in the United States. The main law regulating child labor in the United States is the Fair Labor Standards Act.

103

In general, for non-agricultural jobs, children under fourteen may not be employed. The National Child Labor Committee, an organization dedicated to the abolition of all child labor, was formed in 1904. The National Child Labor Committee published information on the lives and working conditions of young workers, it help to mobitize popular support for state level child labor laws. These laws was designed to keep children in school and out of the paid labor market until a specified age.

Arthur G. Dozier Reform School for Boys (AGDS) operated from January 1, 1900, to June 30, 2011. Throughout its 111-year history, the school gained a reputation for abuse, beatings, rapes, torture and even murder of students by staff.

My research guided me to the finanical records of Dozier, clearly stated to me that the boys were being used at as modern day slaves. Did the National Child Labor Committee ever investigation the modern day slave practices at Dozier Reform School? The school opened it doors six years after the committee was formed. The boys human and civil rights were violated by the state of Florida.

www.ingramcontent.com/pod-product-compliance
Lightning Source LLC
LaVergne TN
LVHW051700080426
835511LV00017B/2655